MICHAEL GIBSON

WEATHER

A PICTURE SCIENCE BOOK

Illustrated by Joseph McEwan

HODDER AND STOUGHTON
LONDON SYDNEY AUCKLAND TORONTO

CONTENTS

British Library Cataloguing in Publication Data

Gibson, Michael
    Weather. – (Picture science books).
    1. Weather – Juvenile literature
    I. Title   II. Series
    551.5   QC981.3

    ISBN 0-340-25202-2

Photographs on pages 7, 21, 24, 26, 30 reproduced with permission of the Controller of Her Majesty's Stationery Office.

The weather is always with us

Since the air we breathe and live in – the atmosphere – completely surrounds the Earth, and since weather changes are the result of changes in the atmosphere, the weather, whether we like it or not, is always with us. It is all about us, all the time.

We do not like it if it is wet and cold and windy when a holiday has been planned. We are pleased if it is calm and warm and sunny, but months of unbroken sunshine can cause problems, for all living things need water in the form of rain if they are to grow. One could say that ideal weather might consist of sunny days, with just the right amount of rain during the night to provide the water needed, but this is very rare. So many different things affect the weather we have: the rotation of the Earth in the first place, and its journey round the Sun, changing the strength of the Sun's rays at different times, and also the length of the days and nights; the amount of heat from the Sun stored in the Earth's surface or in the sea; the mountains and valleys on the Earth's surface; the numbers of trees and plants there are in a certain area, for they give off moisture into the air; the amount of electricity the air contains at any one time, and much else besides.

There are, of course, parts of the Earth where, at set times of the year, there are likely to be hot days for weeks or months on end, or where it is possible to say within a day or two that snow is expected. This is because at least some of the things that affect the weather in these places are not so subject to change. Climbing a mountain takes one higher into the atmosphere, where it is always colder, so snow can be predicted. The more one moves towards the Equator, where the Sun's rays come from right overhead and so are at their strongest, the hotter it will be; the nearer one goes to the Poles, the colder. It is between these two extremes, in the more temperate latitudes between the Poles and the Equator, that the weather is least predictable, but nowhere on Earth is it completely fixed and stable. Tropical storms occur on the Equator, and gales howl in the polar regions.

The most important influence on the world's weather is the Sun. Its rays are felt most strongly at the Equator, where they come from directly overhead.

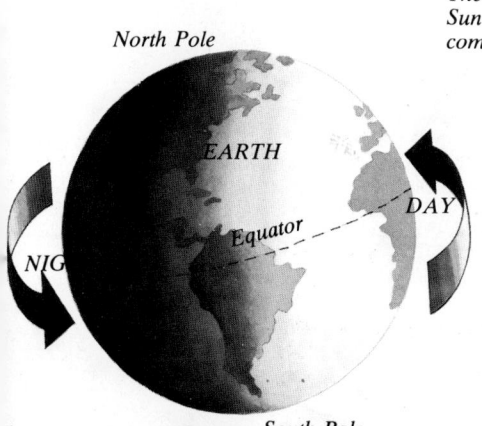

North Pole

EARTH

Equator

DAY

NIG

SUN

South Pole

Weather lore

Because it has such an effect on everyday life, people have since the earliest times tried to predict how the weather was going to change from day to day. In the beginning there were no scientific instruments to help them. Instead, they watched the sky, and gradually began to realise, for instance, that different kinds of clouds were signs of different kinds of weather to come, that an east wind was generally a cold one, or that the temperature changed with the seasons and brought snow and frost in winter. Probably they had little idea why this should be so, but countrymen especially, spending most of their lives out of doors, were guided in the planting and harvesting of their crops by weather signs they saw repeated from year to year.

None of this knowledge was recorded for a long time. It was passed on from one generation to another by word of mouth, and some of the best-known weather signs became everyday sayings and, even later, rhymes and jingles. 'Red sky at night is the shepherd's delight; Red sky at morning is the shepherd's warning' is perhaps the best known, and generally speaking it is true. If at dawn the red rays of the Sun shine on clouds coming in from the west, rain may well follow during the day. By evening, the Sun is in the west, and its rays light up clouds moving away to the east.

A red sunset often means good weather the next day. (R. N. Hughes)

Most of the popular sayings have some truth in them, though none of them is completely reliable. 'The north wind doth blow, and we shall have snow', 'When the wind is in the east, it is neither fit for man nor beast', 'Mackerel sky, not long wet, not long dry', 'Rain before seven, fine before eleven', and 'A ring around the moon brings rain upon you soon' are others. In the course of reading this book, the reasons why these sayings may often be true should become clear.

IONOSPHERE

STRATOSPHERE

10 miles above the Earth

TROPOPAUSE

5 miles above the Earth

TROPOSPHERE

Sea level

The Earth's atmosphere

The atmosphere that surrounds the Earth is actually made up of a number of layers, though as they are all formed from mixtures of gases one cannot see any dividing line between them. Up to a height of something like 45 miles above the level of the sea there is about 78 per cent nitrogen and 21 per cent oxygen, the rest being small quantities of other gases such as carbon dioxide and argon. Up to a height of roughly 5 miles, water vapour is mixed in with them as well, drawn up into the atmosphere when the heat of the Sun causes it to evaporate from the sea, rivers and lakes.

This lower, 5-mile layer of the atmosphere is called the *troposphere*, and it is in it that clouds and rain form. The higher one goes in the troposphere the colder it becomes, the temperature dropping about 0.6 °C per 100 m., which has a great effect on the weather as will be seen. Beyond the troposphere comes a boundary layer known as the *tropopause* and then, at a height varying between about 11 miles over the Equator to 5 miles over the North and South Poles, the *stratosphere* begins. In this there are no clouds and the temperature remains constant all the time, though it is very cold.

Farther away from the Earth still is the *ionosphere*, where the composition of gases is different, but it is the troposphere on which we must concentrate, for it is there that things happen that cause the changes in the weather.

Heat and cold

The three main things which cause a change in the weather are a rise or fall in the *temperature* of the atmosphere, a change of air or *atmospheric pressure*, and an alteration in its moisture content or *humidity*. More often than not, all three change at once and in meteorology, as the study and recording of the weather is called, these changes have to be measured if forecasts are to be made.

Taking temperature first, this is measured by making use of the fact that metals expand when they are heated, and contract when the temperature drops. The amount they expand or contract for a given temperature rise is always the same for any one metal. Though a liquid, mercury is a metal and it is used in an instrument called a *thermometer* to measure temperature changes. It is contained in a bulb at the end of a long, narrow glass tube, and when the temperature rises the mercury expands in the bulb and is pushed up the tube. This is marked with a scale showing the degrees of temperature rise, the reading being taken at the top of the mercury column. For very low temperature measurements, when mercury would freeze, alcohol, which has a lower freezing point, is used instead.

For the really accurate measurement of air temperature which is needed in meteorology, it is not enough simply to put a thermometer out of doors. The reason for this can be seen if you imagine putting your hand on a flat stone which has been lying in the sun. The stone will be much hotter than the air surrounding it, and if a thermometer were put out in the sun the same thing would happen. The temperature of the mercury and the glass of the thermometer would be greater than that of the air, and the reading much higher than it should be in consequence. To get over this problem, meteorological thermometers are kept in small wooden structures which look rather like beehives on legs. In these, they are sheltered from direct sunlight, but air can pass freely through the sides, which are slatted, like a venetian blind.

Above: *A thermometer, showing temperatures in both °Fahrenheit (left) and °Centigrade or Celsius (right). It works on the principle that metal (in this case mercury) expands when heated.*

Right: *Meteorological thermometers are kept sheltered from direct sunlight in slatted wooden boxes, called Stevenson Screens.*

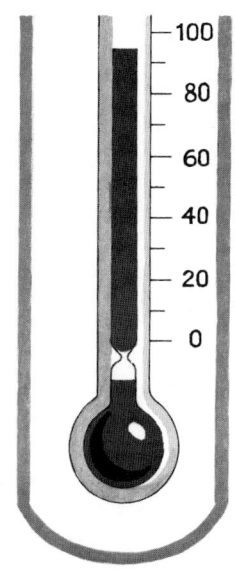

Maximum thermometer. The top of the mercury shows the maximum temperature reached. The mercury has contracted into the bulb, leaving a gap below the constriction.

Minimum thermometer. The index, or pointer, moves down with the alcohol used in this type of thermometer and stays at the lowest point reached.

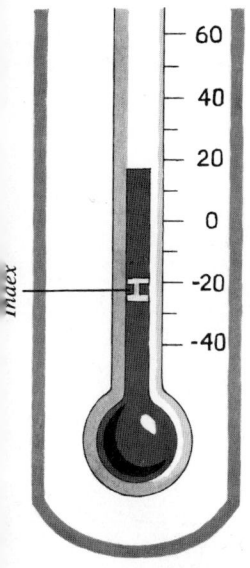

If proper records are to be kept, it is necessary to know the maximum and minimum temperatures which have been reached during the course of a night or day, but as one cannot sit watching a thermometer all the time, special ones are used. A *maximum thermometer* has a constriction in the glass tube, through which mercury is forced by expansion in the bulb. The top of the mercury column moves up the scale to the point where the highest temperature is reached and remains there, for the combined forces of contraction on cooling and of gravity are not sufficient to bring it back down through the constriction. The thermometer used by a doctor is of this kind, and the mercury must be shaken back down into the bulb.

A *minimum thermometer*, which uses alcohol rather than mercury, has a small metal 'index' or 'pointer' in the tube. This is drawn down by the surface tension of the alcohol as the temperature drops until the lowest reading is reached. If the temperature rises again, the alcohol flows up past the 'index', leaving it to show just how cold it has been.

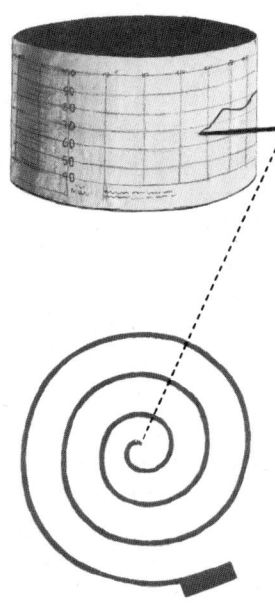

Coiled metal strip in thermograph, linked to pen marking the drum.

Thermograph (HMSO)

To make a continuous record of temperature changes, a *thermograph* is employed instead of thermometers. In this, there is a coiled strip of two metals with different rates of expansion, which are fused together. A greater rate of expansion or contraction, with a rise or fall in temperature of the inner metal in the coil, causes it to wind itself more tightly or to unwind. An arm with a special pen at the end of it is linked to the coil and moves as the coil moves, tracing a graph of temperature changes on a revolving drum, round which a strip of paper marked with a temperature scale has been clipped.

Air pressure and the weather

The air is all around us and, though we do not normally feel it, it is exerting a pressure on us and on everything else. This can, perhaps, be more easily understood if one compares the air to the water in the sea. The deeper one goes in the sea, the greater the pressure because there is more weight of water above us. Submarines have to be specially built to withstand these pressures, and a man who could swim quite happily on the surface would be crushed if he descended far enough without protection.

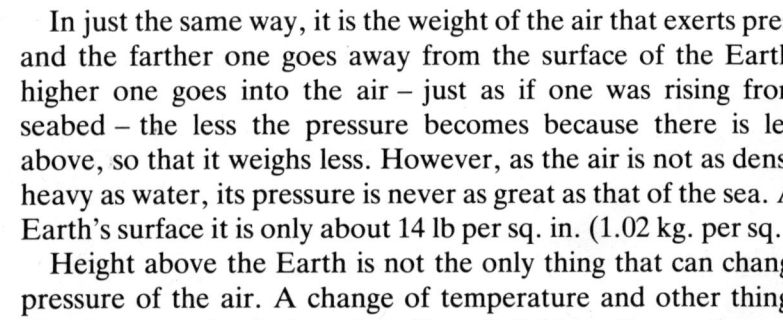

Low air pressure

High air pressure

Low water pressure

SEA LEVEL

High water pressure

In just the same way, it is the weight of the air that exerts pressure, and the farther one goes away from the surface of the Earth, the higher one goes into the air – just as if one was rising from the seabed – the less the pressure becomes because there is less air above, so that it weighs less. However, as the air is not as dense and heavy as water, its pressure is never as great as that of the sea. At the Earth's surface it is only about 14 lb per sq. in. (1.02 kg. per sq. cm.).

Height above the Earth is not the only thing that can change the pressure of the air. A change of temperature and other things can alter it, too, and to find out the effect of all this on the weather – and it does affect it greatly – measurements of changes in atmospheric pressure must be made.

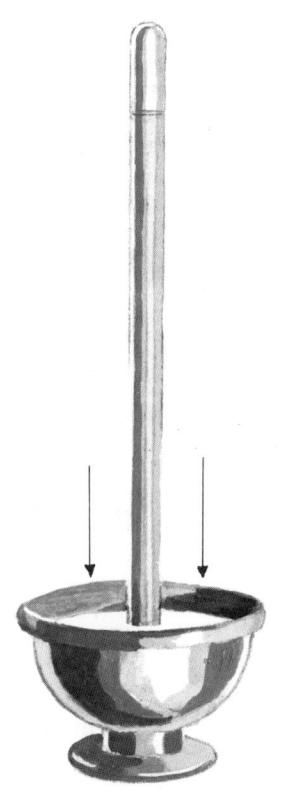

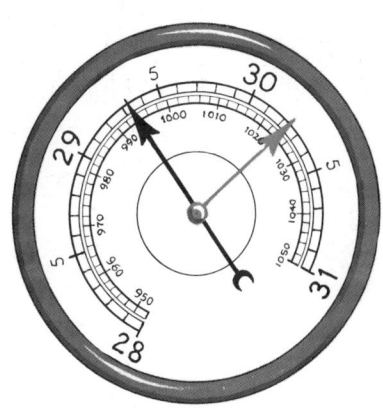

Left: *Torricelli's experiment –
atmospheric pressure holds the mercury
in the tube. Try the experiment yourself
with a milk bottle over a sink of water.*

Right: *A modern barometer, showing
atmospheric pressure both in inches of
mercury and in millibars. The light-
coloured arrow gives the previous
reading.*

It was an Italian scientist, Evangelista Torricelli, living over 300 years ago, who discovered that the air exerted pressure on things around it. The experiment by which he proved this used exactly the same principle as that of a modern barometer. Torricelli took a long, straight, narrow tube with one end sealed, filled it with mercury and, taking care that the mercury did not run out of the tube, turned it upside down and put the open end in a bowl, also filled with mercury. That in the tube stayed there, a column 30 inches high, because the pressure of the air on the surface of the mercury in the bowl kept it there. No air could get into the top of the tube to balance this and force it out.

A variation in the air pressure would affect the height of the mercury column in the tube, and a modern *barometer* has a dial linked to it so that this can be measured. It does not, in fact, use a bowl of mercury, as this would be easily spilled. Instead, the bottom, open end of the tube is bent upwards in the shape of a 'U', and air pressure acts on this. A float on the surface of the mercury at the top of the closed end of the tube is attached to a pointer, which moves round a dial showing pressure changes. In meteorology, pressure is measured in units called *millibars*, each one equal to 1.02 grams per square centimetre. There has to be some adjustment made to take into account the temperature of the mercury, as this can affect the accuracy of the reading.

An *aneroid barometer* measures pressure in a different way. It consists of a small, concertina-like capsule of very thin metal, inside which there is a partial vacuum. An increase in air pressure squeezes the capsule; a decrease and it expands, the movement once again being linked to a dial from which readings can be taken. This is the way the altimeter of an aeroplane works. The higher the aeroplane goes, the lower the pressure reading, which is converted by the altimeter into the height in feet. At 18,000 ft, for instance, pressure would be about half what it would be at sea level.

*How an aneroid barometer
works – high pressure expands
the concertina-like vacuum
box, low pressure contracts it.
The movement affects the
spring, which is connected to
the pointer on the dial.*

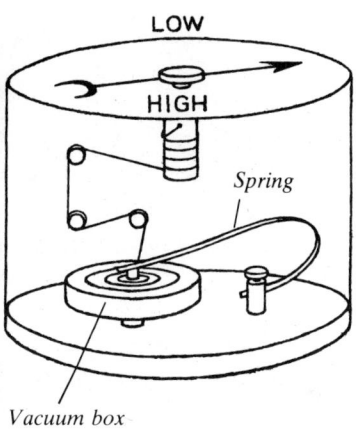

Vacuum box

9

The water in the air

As we have seen, evaporation, mainly from the sea and other large stretches of water but also from the leaves of plants and trees (transpiration) and from rain-sodden earth, carries water into the air in the form of an invisible vapour. It is the effect of changing temperatures on this vapour that is the cause of clouds forming, and of rain, sleet, snow, fog and mists; so the water vapour in the air has a great deal to do with the kind of weather we have.

There is a limit to the amount of water vapour which air can hold, and this varies with its temperature. Hot air can hold much more water than cold, but however hot it is there will always be a maximum amount. When this maximum is reached, the air is said to be saturated; but as a rule the air only holds quite a small proportion of the water vapour needed to reach saturation point at any given temperature. The difference between the amount of water vapour actually there and what is, in theory, possible, is known to meteorologists as the *relative humidity*.

The amount of vapour is measured in terms of its weight in grams per cubic metre of air. If the air is completely saturated with water, the relative humidity is said to be 100 per cent. If the weight of vapour were halved (the temperature remaining unchanged), the relative humidity would be halved also, becoming 50 per cent. In muggy weather, when clothes feel damp and clammy, the relative humidity is high. Perspiration clings to our bodies as it cannot evaporate into air already heavy with vapour. In contrast, a cold, clear, frosty day feels fresh and invigorating. If we breathe out, we can see our breath,

Cloud

Cold air

Evaporation of water into atmosphere

Evaporation of water from the Earth's surface creates invisible vapour in the air. The amount of water vapour the air can hold varies with its temperature . . .

. . . which is why we sweat on hot, humid days . . .

. . . and why warm, damp breath can be seen as a cloud in cold, crisp weather.

Warm air

Air cooled by ground so dew forms

Cold ground

which is warm and damp. The water vapour in it condenses as the air cools it, so that we can see it as we can see a cloud, and then disperses into air that is comparatively dry. If it were misty as well as frosty, our breath would remain visible, mingling with the mist and not dispersing in the same way.

As we have seen, the amount of vapour air can hold becomes less as the temperature drops, so that air that was reasonably dry to begin with will in time reach its saturation point if the temperature drops steadily. The excess of water is then deposited on surrounding objects. Dew is formed in this way when the air cools at night, and the point at which this happens is known to the weathermen as the *dew point*. The misting of windows occurs if the temperature of the glass is lower than that of the surrounding air, because it cools the air immediately next to it until its dew point is reached and condensation (misting) occurs.

The simplest way to measure the amount of water vapour in the air is to use a *dry-bulb* and a *wet-bulb thermometer*. The dry-bulb one is a normal thermometer, and the wet-bulb one is identical, except that the bulb is contained in a small, muslin bag. This is kept moist by a wick drawing water up from a container. Evaporation of water into the air from the muslin bag lowers the temperature of the wet-bulb, and the relative humidity is calculated from the difference in the temperature readings of the two thermometers. If the air is saturated, no evaporation can take place from the muslin, and both thermometers will show the same temperature.

Dew is formed when the earth cools at night, lowering the temperature of the air above it; colder air cannot hold so much water, and the excess is deposited ('condenses') on surrounding objects.

Dry bulb and wet bulb thermometers. The wet bulb is tied in a wet muslin bag. Evaporation of the water into the atmosphere lowers the temperature of the bulb, and relative humidity can be calculated from comparison of the two thermometer readings.

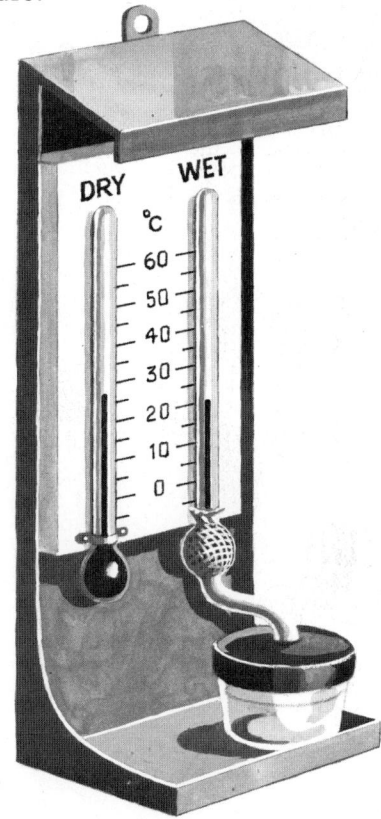

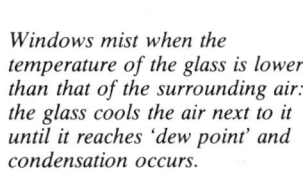

Windows mist when the temperature of the glass is lower than that of the surrounding air: the glass cools the air next to it until it reaches 'dew point' and condensation occurs.

Draught

Hot air rises. Hot air goes up the chimney (above) and cold air rushes to take its place. By the same principle (right), the Sun warms the Earth's surface and part of its energy is reflected back. This warms the air, which rises, and cold air rushes to take its place, causing winds.

Movement in the atmosphere

Having said something about changes in temperature, pressure and humidity in the atmosphere, the next step is to find out how the weather is affected by them. 'Hot air rises' is a well-known saying, and this can be taken as a starting point.

Hot air rising carries smoke from a fire up the chimney. Cooler air from below is drawn in to take its place, which can cause a draught if the fireplace is not properly designed. On a much larger scale, the Sun shines on the Earth's surface and part of its energy, in the form of heat, is absorbed by the Earth. A proportion is, however, reflected or radiated back into the atmosphere, warming the air. The warm air begins to rise, and since it is no longer there, the pressure in the space it occupied is lowered and cooler air rushes in to take its place. This causes a wind, which can be thought of as an enormous draught.

Gliding birds (above) soar on rising warm air or 'thermals'. Glider pilots (opposite) look for cumulus clouds, which are created by rising, moist thermals which have reached saturation point.

Sun's heat energy

Warm air rises

Since the higher one goes in the atmosphere the colder it gets, the rising air, which is known as a *thermal*, is gradually cooled. It will eventually reach a height where it is of the same temperature as that surrounding it and movement will cease. If further cooling takes place it will descend once more.

If the upward current, or thermal, consists of moist air, as the temperature drops gradually so will the relative humidity increase. It can hold less water vapour, and when the saturation point is reached the vapour will be condensed into millions of minute droplets, not heavy enough to fall as rain, but visible from the Earth as a cloud. Clouds formed in this way are known as *cumulus clouds*, and are shaped like gigantic cauliflowers, usually with a flattish, darker base. They may be thousands of feet high, reaching right up into the boundary layer of the tropopause.

A glider pilot will always be on the look-out for cumulus clouds because he knows that there will be up-currents of air beneath them on which he can soar for long periods, passing, if he wishes to cover long distances, from one cloud and one thermal to another neighbouring one. Soaring birds also use these thermals, in which they can float on outstretched wings with little or no effort at all.

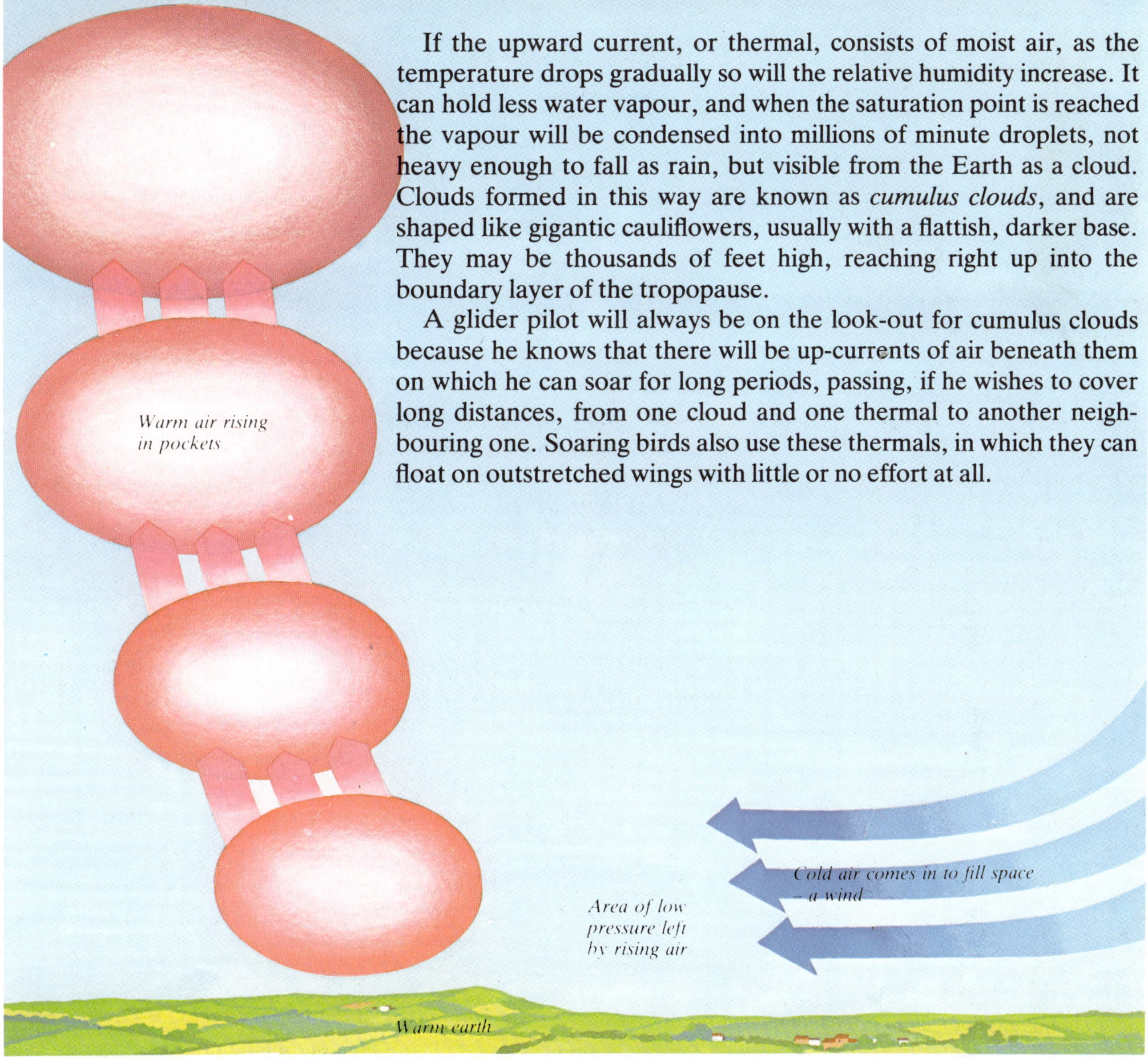

Warm air rising in pockets

Cold air comes in to fill space — a wind

Area of low pressure left by rising air

Warm earth

Since the evaporation of water and thermal currents both depend on warmth, except in countries nearest to the Equator (where hot weather is more or less constant) the amount of evaporation and the rising and falling of currents of air will vary continually. This will be so, not only from one part of the year to another, but in places it will vary daily and even hour by hour. This is one of the things that makes weather forecasting so difficult, for the Sun will come and go from behind clouds, alternately warming and cooling the Earth. However, taken over a period as long as a year, in each part of the world there is a fairly constant water cycle. In other words, the amount of water drawn up from the Earth into the atmosphere, to return as rain and drain back into the sea and lakes by means of rivers and streams, remains much the same.

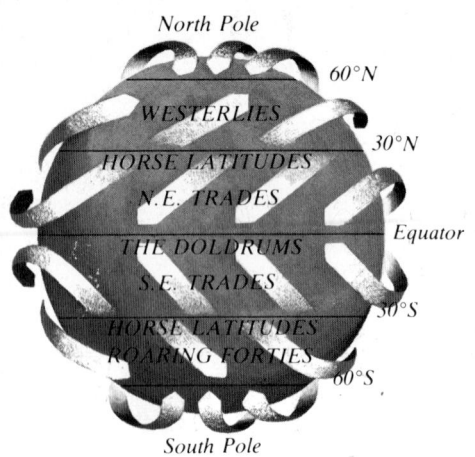

The World's most important winds.

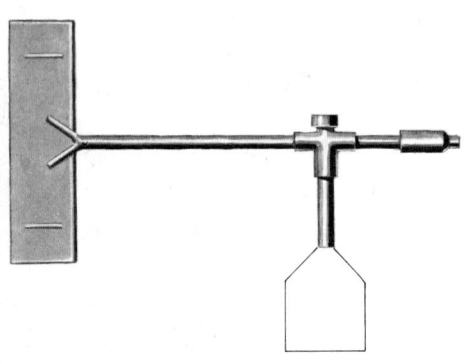

Pressure tube anemometer.

Cup anemometer.

The wind

It might be thought that, as the temperature at the Equator is always high, and that at the North and South Poles low, the wind would always blow from the Poles towards the Equator. Hot air over the Equator would rise and draw in cold air from the Poles to replace it.

This would be so if the Earth were stationary in space, but its rotation actually causes the winds in the south to swing first west and then east, and those in the north to swing first east and then west, which is due to pressure differences built up by the winds themselves. And in certain areas and at certain times of year, the direction of these winds can be changed yet again as they pass over large areas of land or sea, differing in their temperatures, though not as much as the difference between the Poles and the Equator.

It is difficult when out for a walk on a gusty day to see any pattern in the way the wind blows. Its strength will vary from moment to moment, and it may well seem to be coming from all directions at once. This is largely due to the fact that it is not blowing over completely flat and level country which is of an absolutely uniform temperature. Hills or mountains can deflect it upwards and then downwards again on the other side into valleys; trees and buildings can cause it to slow down or to swirl round them, much as the incoming tide will swirl round rocks on the sea shore.

However, despite all these variations, there will be one main direction in which the wind is blowing at any one time. It will be a north wind (coming from the north), an east wind (coming from the east), or a west wind and so on, generally moving from a cold area towards a warmer one. These areas may be vast, whole countries or continents, or they may be seas or oceans. In winter, the northern seas will be colder than the land mass of Europe and 'the north wind doth blow'. However, as the land gradually cools, the winds will come more from the east, blowing towards the Gulf Stream, which is a current of warm water in the Atlantic that flows up the coast of western Europe, heating the air above it. In the summer, the land heats up more rapidly than the sea, and the winds change to west winds, blowing in the opposite direction.

In other parts of the world there will be different prevailing winds according to how the land and the sea lie in relation one to another. But the principles will be the same, and in Australia, for instance, the north wind will be a warm one from the tropics, drawn south by the very dry hot air rising above the baking central desert regions.

Hurricanes, cyclones and *typhoons* are names used in different parts of the world for what are virtually the same things, tropical storms. They are caused by areas of very low pressure not more than 300–400 miles wide, into which wind rushes at tremendous speed,

Mountains, seas, even buildings can all affect the way a wind blows.

usually causing a great deal of damage on land and wrecking ships at sea.

Wind speed can be measured accurately either by a *pressure tube* or by a *cup anemometer*. In the former, a tube with an open end on a swivel mounting is kept pointing into the wind by a vane. The wind pressure in the tube is converted into wind speed, which is shown on a dial. A cup anemometer has cup or cone-shaped revolving vanes, which turn in the wind. In this case the speed at which they revolve indicates wind speed, much in the way a car speedometer shows how fast it is going.

However, for general use in calculating wind speed something called the *Beaufort Scale* is used, and this depends on the effect the wind has on everyday objects you can see. The diagram shows just how it works.

The Beaufort Scale measures wind force by its effect on every-day objects, without the aid of instruments.

0 Calm	1 Light air	2 Light breeze	3 Gentle breeze	4 Moderate breeze	5 Fresh breeze	6 Strong breeze	7 Moderate gale	8 Fresh gale	9 Strong gale	10 Whole gale	11 Storm	12 Hurricane
Smoke rises vertically	Smoke drifts	Weather vane moved	Flags extended	Dust and loose paper moved	Small trees sway	Large branches in motion	Whole trees in motion	Twigs broken off trees	Large branches break, roof tiles lifted	Trees uprooted, roofs damaged	Wide-spread damage	Disaster

15

The Sun

The lengths of days and nights vary with the seasons. In summer, the days are longer and the nights shorter. In winter it is the other way round, due to the constantly changing position of the Earth as it moves round the Sun, turning at the same time about its own axis. The North and South Poles never face directly towards the Sun. Its rays always strike them at an angle, so that its heat energy is greatly reduced, and in addition the white snow and ice reflect much of what energy there is away from themselves, so little is absorbed and stored in the way it is elsewhere.

Sun's rays strike at angle; most heat is deflected by ice and snow

Clouds prevent some heat ever reaching Earth, also trap some heat reflected back from Earth

Sun's rays (short wave)

Reflected heat (long wave) warms atmosphere

Equator: Sun directly overhead – very hot

Some heat reflected back by water vapour and carbon dioxide in atmosphere

As one moves round the Earth towards the Equator, the Sun becomes more nearly overhead and it is much hotter. However, in general, the length of time the Sun shines, and hence the amount of heat it passes to the Earth, depends on the time of year. The longer the days, the more heat the Earth's surface will be able to absorb.

Since a change in the temperature of the atmosphere has such an effect on the weather, the way this comes about is worth going into a little more fully. Rather strangely, as we have seen already, it is not the heat radiated by the Sun that actually warms the air, at least not directly. Most of the heat energy, by what is known as *short-wave*

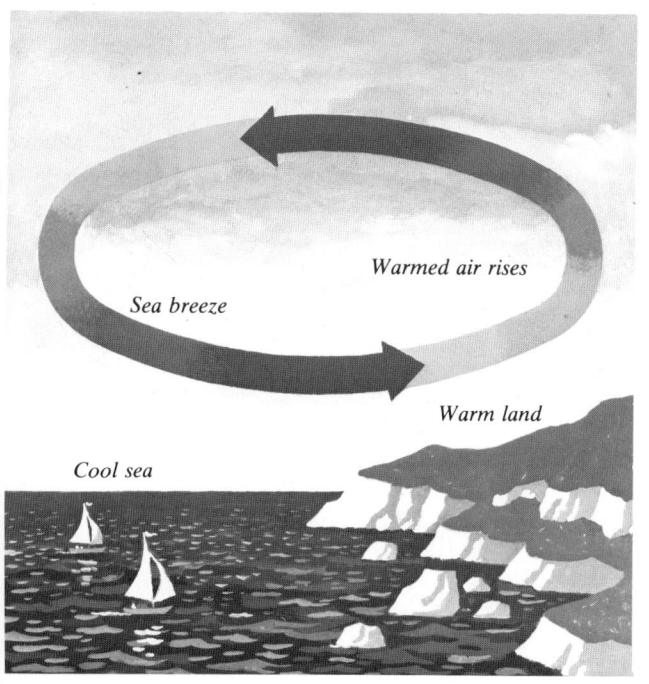

Sea breeze

Warmed air rises

Warm land

Cool sea

Warmed air rises

Land breeze

Warmer sea

Land cools

By day, the sea is cooler than the land, which absorbs the Sun's heat more quickly. At night, the land quickly loses its heat, while the sea retains it and is warmer. So by day breezes tend to blow from the sea, by night from the land.

Campbell-Stokes sunshine recorder focuses the Sun's rays through a glass ball on to a marked card. Charring on the card shows when and how strongly the Sun was shining.

radiation, passes straight through the air to the Earth's surface. There, part of it is absorbed and part, now changed to *long-wave radiation*, is reflected back again, warming the air, and particularly the water vapour and carbon dioxide in it. These in their turn reflect some of the heat back once more to the Earth. The sea absorbs the Sun's heat more slowly than the land, and so it warms up more slowly. That is why there tend to be winds off-shore during the night and a breeze from the sea during the day, as well as the prevailing winds of winter and summer.

As the atmosphere always contains some water vapour, dust, smoke particles and often clouds, part of the Sun's energy is reflected back by these into space and never reaches the Earth at all. On the other hand, they also trap some of the heat reflected back from the Earth, and so help to keep the air warm.

The Sun radiates light, in all the colours of the spectrum, as well as heat. The blue of the sky is due to the effect of the blue part of the spectrum on air molecules. Dust particles pick up the reds and yellows, giving spectacular sunsets.

If a magnifying glass is held in strong sunlight and focused on a sheet of paper, the heat will first char and eventually set light to the paper. For measuring the amount of sunshine, the *Campbell-Stokes recorder* makes use of this principle, using a glass ball instead of a magnifying glass. This focuses the Sun's rays on to a card, which is marked off in hours and treated so that it will not actually catch fire, though it will char. It is changed each day, and the charred parts show when the Sun was shining and how strongly.

How clouds are formed

Air pressure is greater nearer the Earth because of the weight of air above it. When warm air rises higher and higher it is gradually cooled, but as it is also under less pressure it expands as well. In doing this, its temperature drops even more rapidly until at length it can hold no more water, its saturation point has been reached, and condensation takes place. The particles of dust with which the atmosphere is filled are often so minute that the eye cannot see them, but it is round these particles that the tiny droplets of water form on condensation. These are themselves so small that they continue to float in the air, but together in a mass they make up the clouds we can see.

Stratus A low layer of cloud of uniform height, which is sometimes broken up into shapeless masses.

Nimbostratus A low, dark grey layer of cloud, usually bringing continuous rain and sometimes snow.

Cumulus Towering clouds several thousand feet high, with irregular, rounded tops, and usually flat or nearly flat bases. They may bring showers.

Cumulonimbus Very large cumulus clouds with dark bases, reaching up into the tropopause. Thunder is likely when they are about.

Stratocumulus A scattered, broken layer of cloud, made up of what resemble flattened cumulus clouds.

Cirrus The highest clouds of all, which may be at heights of 50,000 feet. They are often known as 'mare's tails'. They are made up of ice crystals.

Cirrostratus Very like altostratus but higher. The Sun or Moon shining through them appears to have a halo. They may thicken into altostratus and bring rain.

Cirrocumulus The well-known 'mackerel sky', made up of small, fleecy clouds very high up, forming more or less regular patterns and lines like those on the back of a mackerel.

There are a number of different types of cloud, each with its own name, and how and why each type forms depends to a considerable extent on just how smoothly and evenly warm air masses move upwards, and also on the height they have reached when condensation into clouds takes place. Some of the higher clouds, where the cold is intense, may be formed of ice crystals rather than droplets of water.

If the air rises steadily in very large masses or in unbroken columns, separate, towering white clouds will be formed, with blue sky around them. However, if the air is whirled about as it moves upwards by a gusty wind, the large masses of warm air may be broken up into smaller ones, all jumbled together. When they reach the height at which clouds are formed, they will merge into a continuous cloud layer, and the sky is overcast. There are, as we know, many kinds of cloud formation between these two extremes.

Altostratus A uniform layer of high cloud, through which the Sun shines hazily. This may turn to rain clouds if the layer thickens.

Altocumulus Small, high, light grey clouds which pale in colour towards their edges, often forming lines with blue sky in between.

Rain

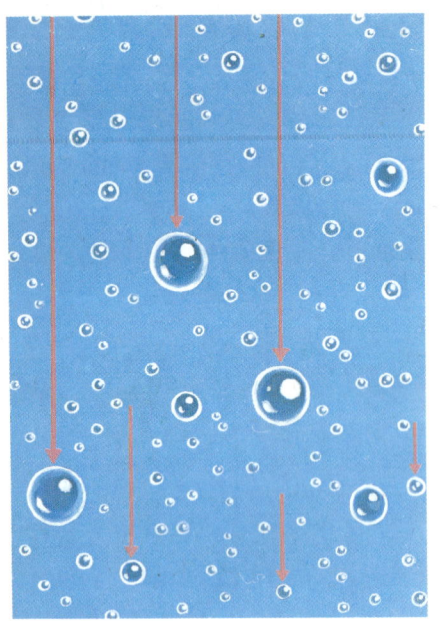

Raindrops forming in a tropical storm. A raindrop can never be more than 5½mm across.

It takes thousands of the droplets of water which go to make up clouds to form one single raindrop, and it might be thought that they would simply merge together to form larger, heavier drops and then fall as rain. It does not, however, happen quite as simply as that. A change in temperature once more plays a part.

When the temperature in a cloud drops to or below freezing point, some of the tiny water droplets freeze. The vapour formed by the remaining droplets condenses on the frozen ones, which at once become much heavier and begin to fall into warmer air. The ice melts, and raindrops are the result, though heavy, tropical rain goes through yet another stage. In it, faster-moving, larger drops gather other, smaller ones on their way down, but just the same there is a maximum size a raindrop can reach. Over about 5½ mm. across, the surface tension of the water will no longer hold it together, and a large drop breaks up into smaller ones once more.

We have seen that rising air cools as it expands. In a column or large pocket of air rising over a comparatively small area to form cumulus clouds, more and more vapour condenses the higher it goes. Eventually there will be showers, though they do not usually last long. Meteorologists call this *convection rain*, because convection means the upward or downward movement of air through a change in its temperature, which is what has occurred here.

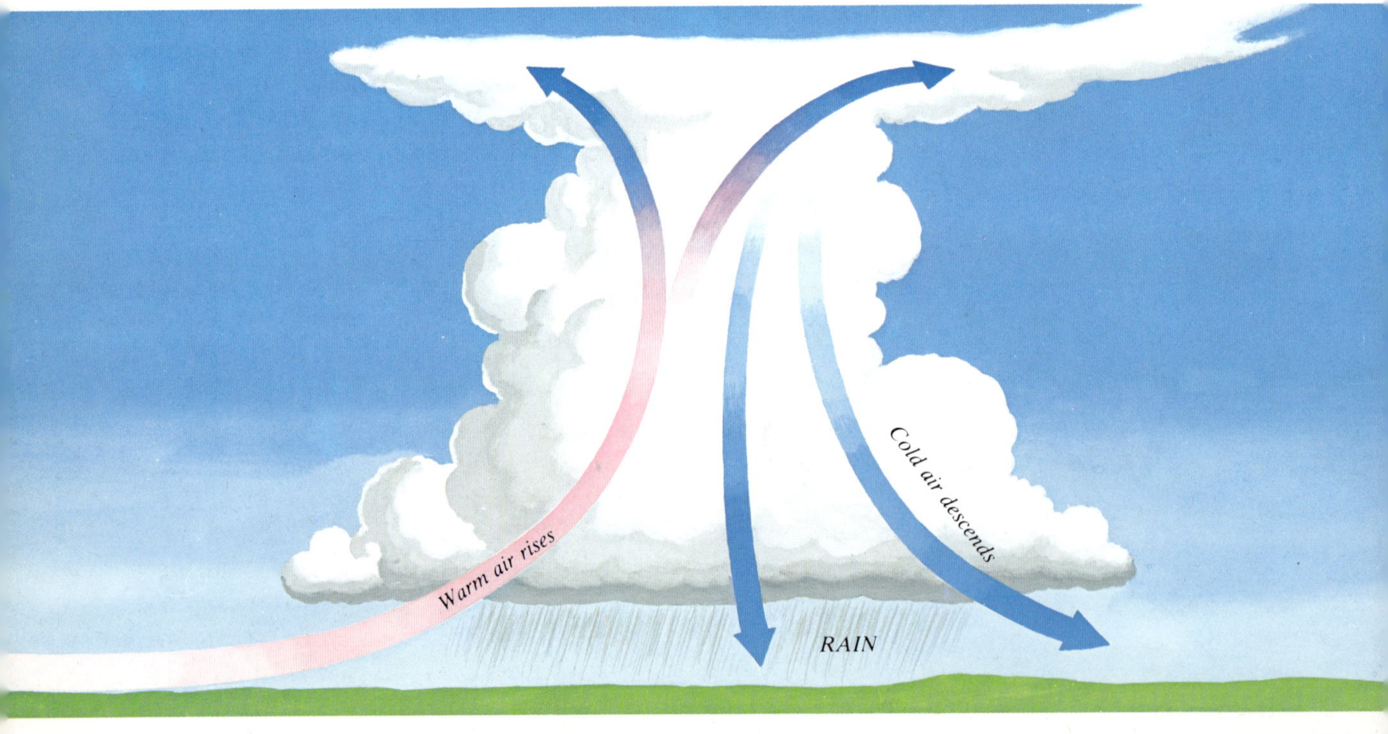

Warm air rises

Cold air descends

RAIN

Convection rainfall.

Damp wind rises and cools   RAIN   NO RAIN

Orographic rainfall.

Measuring rainfall. (HMSO)

Rain over long periods – rainy days – means that warm air has risen over an area perhaps hundreds of miles across, forming a thick layer of altostratus or nimbostratus clouds, and the rain that falls from them is known as *cyclonic*. The third kind of rain is *orographic*, when damp air is blown by the wind upwards over a mountain range, forming rain clouds on the side of the mountains from which the wind comes.

Drizzle is really rain with drops larger than those of the droplets in a cloud but not as large as raindrops. It falls from a height below that from which convection rain would come.

The amount of rainfall is measured in terms of the depth of water it will produce in a given period – say one hour. Some countries record it in millimeters and some in inches, but it takes many, many hours of very heavy rain to produce even as shallow a depth as one inch (25 mm.).

The simplest raingauge consists of a funnel into which the rain falls, passing from it into a bottle or other container. After a regular fixed period, the water from the container is poured into a special measuring glass. Markings on the side of this take into account the difference between the area of the top of the funnel (the area on which the rain has actually fallen) and the diameter of the measuring glass, so that the real depth of rain can be seen straight away. More complicated gauges, using what is basically the same principle but recording the results on a chart fixed to a revolving drum, register rainfall over long periods.

21

Hail, snow, sleet, ice and frost

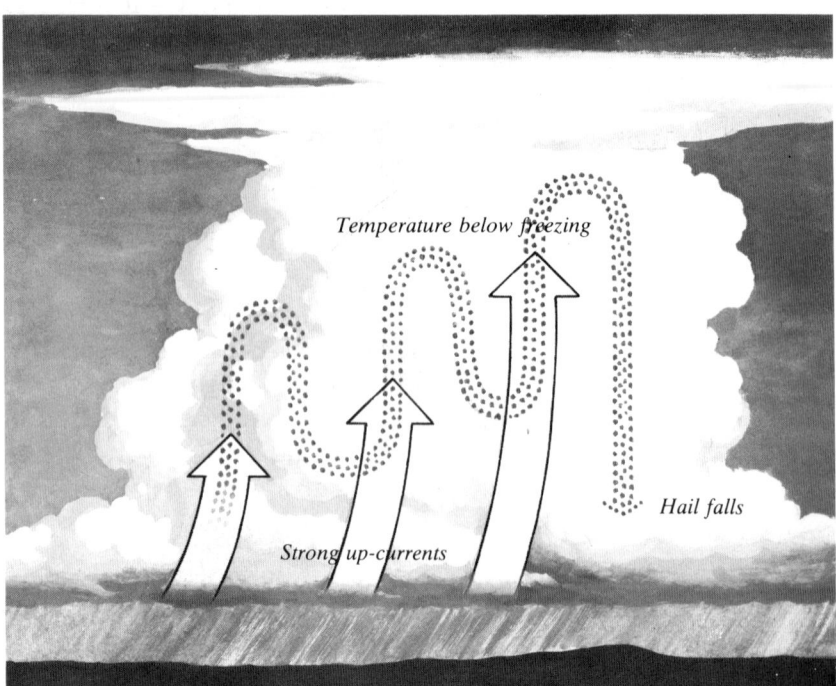

Temperature below freezing

Strong up-currents

Hail falls

Hailstones are ice crystals which have been repeatedly tossed up by strong winds into freezing temperatures, collecting successive coverings of ice until they become so heavy that they fall to earth.

Snowflakes are always six-sided, but occur in an enormous variety of shapes.

Although *hailstones* are formed of ice, they can fall on quite a warm day, though they melt quickly on the ground. Most of them are quite small and only damage such fragile things as flowers. However, much larger ones, which are not uncommon in America and parts of the European continent, can destroy crops and smash the glass of greenhouses. They are formed when raindrops at the base of a towering thundercloud, instead of falling, are lifted upwards in a strong air current to a height where they freeze, and then begin to drop downwards, gathering ice crystals and moisture as they do so. Further currents of air whisk them up yet again, and this sequence can be repeated several times, so that they grow steadily in size. Finally they do head for the Earth and we have hail.

Snowflakes consist of a number of ice crystals and are formed in clouds where the temperature is well below freezing point. They will only fall to the ground as flakes if the temperature of the air through which they come down is also below freezing point; otherwise they would simply melt into rain. If the air is very cold indeed, the flakes will remain small and powdery, and the snow when it lies on the ground will not stick together. It will not, for instance, make snowballs. If, on the other hand, the temperature of the air is a little above freezing point, there may be some melting of the falling flakes. Small ones come together to make larger, wetter ones, and on the ground these can be compressed, making it slippery.

22

Measuring snowfall.

The depth of snow fall is measured very simply by means of a pole which is driven vertically into the ground, and which is marked off in inches or centimetres. However, a reading must be taken quite often – at least once a day – for the depth of the snow can change without more falling. A certain amount may melt if the air becomes warmer for an hour or two or if the Sun shines, or the snow can be compressed to a lesser depth by its own weight.

Sleet is a mixture of rain and snow, and falls when the air temperature is too low for pure rain and too high for pure snow.

Ice forming on ponds and puddles simply means that the temperature of the air and the earth surrounding it is below that at which water freezes, but more serious and dangerous for cars and other users of roads is *black ice*, because it cannot easily be seen. It can be formed when rain falls through a very cold layer of air near the ground, and goes through a process known as *supercooling*. This means that the temperature of the drops actually goes below freezing point, but they still stay liquid. However, the instant they reach the ground they do freeze into a thin film of ice, which is almost invisible.

A winter scene. (Barnaby's Picture Library)

As we have seen when discussing humidity, if a night is calm and clear, the ground will cool more quickly than the air, and dew will be formed. If the temperature is low enough, the dew turns to ice crystals, and we have what we call a *white frost* or *hoar frost*.

23

Fog and mist

Foggy weather can cause more problems, at least to anyone who wishes to move about, even to someone walking, than any other kind. Radar, in which radio waves are sent out and 'bounce' back from an object which cannot actually be seen but will show up on the radar screen, can be fitted in ships and aeroplanes. How far the object is away can be calculated by the time the 'echo' of the radio waves takes to come back, but the time is yet to come when people can carry their own radar when walking. One can still bump into a lamp post in fog.

Fog is quite simply a cloud on the ground. It occurs when the air is still, the temperature of the Earth is lower than that of the air near it, and condensation takes place as the air becomes saturated. *Smog* is a particularly unpleasant kind of fog in which the droplets of water condense on the multitude of particles of smoke or chemicals which are already in the air, and which would normally be blown away. The weight of the water round each particle keeps them at a low level and prevents them dispersing. *Mist* is just a thin fog.

Fogs tend to form mainly in low-lying areas because the cold air which forms them is heavier than warm and sinks to the lowest level it can find. One can see this when standing on a hill, looking down on fog or mist covering the countryside below. On the other hand, *hill fogs* can also occur when a damp wind or air current blows up a cool hillside, and then the condensation of the moisture takes place at a much higher level. *Sea mists* form round the coasts when the temperature of the sea and land are different, making that of the air immediately above each different, too. Warm, moist air from the land, mixing with cooler air over the sea, will result in a sea mist.

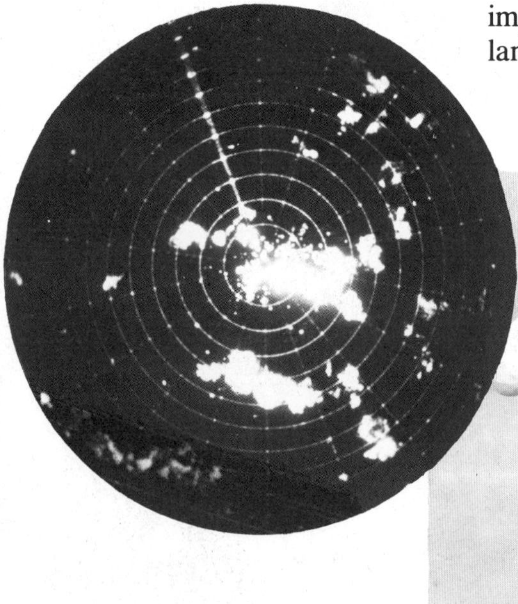

Radar image of heavy showers (HMSO)

Radar sends out radio waves which 'bounce' back from obstructions they meet.

Hill fog.

Sea mist.

Freezing fog – fog when the air temperature is below freezing point – can contain supercooled water droplets of the kind that make black ice. The minute that these touch something such as the branch of a tree or a telegraph wire, they will form a layer of ice over it. This will get thicker and thicker unless there is a thaw, and its weight may, in time, snap off the branch or bring wires down.

To a weatherman, mist becomes fog when he cannot see anything that is more than 1,000 metres away. The density of a fog is measured purely by what can be seen and how far away it is. A weather station will pick a group of trees or perhaps a building and find out how far it is away. Say that its distance is half a mile away from the weather station, when it vanishes from sight in a fog the visibility is said to be half a mile. It is a pity that everything else cannot be measured as simply as this, but the method cannot, of course, be used at night. Instead, a lamp of known brightness is placed permanently at a fixed distance from the station. The strength of the light as it shines through the fog, which grows less as the fog becomes thicker, can be recorded electronically, and converted into the distance one could see if it were daylight.

At a weather station, distances to familiar landmarks will be measured, so that density of fog, when it occurs, can be calculated.

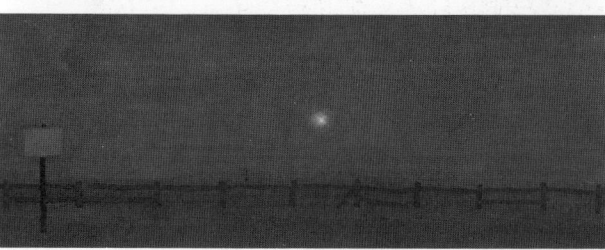

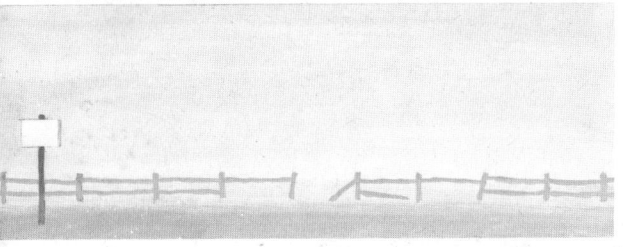

Thunder and lightning

Thunderstorms come about when large masses of warm and very damp air move upwards with great speed to heights which can sometimes be greater than 30,000 ft. Understandably, this causes a tremendous disturbance of the surrounding atmosphere, huge cumulonimbus clouds are formed with dark, lowering bases, and heavy rain and hail may fall from them, accompanied by lightning and the roll of thunder.

Forked lightning. (P. J. Cutting)

Lightning happens when turbulent conditions in a cloud break up raindrops, causing tiny electrical discharges.

Plotting the movement of a thunderstorm. (HMSO)

Sheet lightning. (W. H. Mills)

As would be expected, there are water drops and ice particles forming in the clouds, but they do not come down at once as rain or hail. Hail, as we know, has an up-and-down existence in a cloud's air currents, but in a thundercloud this is carried a stage further. Hail and drops of water are whirled about to such an extent that the raindrops are actually broken up, causing tiny electrical discharges. Combined together, these charges are powerful enough to overcome the insulation which the air would normally give, and flashes of lightning, within the cloud, from cloud to cloud, or from cloud to ground, are the result.

If the light of these flashes is diffused by clouds or comes from a great distance, it is seen as *sheet lightning*. Flashes of *forked lightning* will be much closer and move with great speed – like lightning! – through the air. They do not always reach the ground, but when they do they tend to head for such things as tall buildings or trees, objects in other words which are sticking up a good way above the surface of the Earth. Buildings have lightning conductors to carry the

ightning conductor.

n halo (corona).

electricity safely to the Earth, but trees do not, so it is unwise to shelter under them in a thunderstorm, however heavy the rain.

Tremendous heat is generated by a flash of lightning, which causes the air to expand and then contract again very rapidly. This sets up sound waves in the atmosphere, which are the sometimes quite terrifying, but actually quite harmless, noises of a thunderstorm. If you count the number of seconds between a lightning flash and the clap of thunder which will follow, and divide the seconds by five, the answer will tell you how many miles away the storm is, as sound travels about one mile in five seconds.

Two or more weather stations working together and using special aerials can say exactly where a thunderstorm is, even though it is many miles away. If bearings from each station are plotted on the same chart, the point where they intersect shows the location of the storm. By taking new bearings at regular intervals, they can see in which direction the storm is moving.

Rainbows and Sun haloes

Thunder does not occur very frequently. Special conditions in the atmosphere are needed for it, and for other things as well, which are much less unpleasant. Nothing could be more peaceful and attractive than a rainbow or the halo of light one sometimes sees around the Sun on a hazy day. The latter is caused by the Sun's rays shining on ice crystals in the haze, but with a rainbow they shine on raindrops with an unusual effect. The drops act in the same way as a prism, separating the colours of the spectrum in the rays, and if we could see a whole rainbow it would be a complete circle. However, the centre is on a direct line between the centre of the Sun and the centre of the Earth, and as we are on the Earth's surface, we can never see more than a part of it.

27

Forecasting the weather

Radio-sonde transmits information on air pressure, temperature and humidity.

Free-flying pilot balloon, tracked by radar for information on air movements.

People very often complain about the weather forecast. It rains when it should be dry, or it is cloudy when the Sun was expected to shine, but what has been said so far will have shown how difficult it is, even with modern scientific instruments, to say what the weather will do more than a few hours ahead. The Sun shines through the vast mass of the atmosphere that surrounds the Earth, constantly changing its temperature by its reflected heat, constantly changing its pressure and the amount of moisture in it, keeping it always in motion. Things can alter very rapidly, and the lowering of the air pressure in one part of a country can affect places hundreds of miles away. The air flows back and forth and up and down, bringing clouds, rain, fog, thunder, frost and all the rest. Days that follow one another are rarely the same.

To try to forecast the weather in a country even as small as the United Kingdom, it is necessary for the weathermen to know what is happening far beyond its coastlines, way out into the Atlantic ocean and on the continent of Europe. Special weather ships at sea and other ships as well, and weather stations on land all over the world, send in reports four times a day of conditions in their areas to central control points in the countries of the world. Free-flying balloons, each carrying an instrument known as a *radio-sonde*, transmit data on the temperature, humidity and pressure from up to twenty miles above the Earth. Other pilot balloons are watched through special sighting instruments which record their movement, and through this the speed of the winds in the upper atmosphere is known. Satellites orbiting the Earth carry recording instruments, and from the height at which they fly can photograph cloud formations over a whole continent, and note how they are changing from hour to hour. These photographs, together with weather maps showing what may be expected to happen in individual countries, are shown on our television screens, and the maps on their own appear in newspapers.

The world network of weather observing stations. (WMO, Geneva)

However, complicated as these maps or charts may seem, they are actually very much simplified forms of the ones which are prepared at the weather centres. These would be impossible for anyone who has not been specially trained to understand, and contain much information only the experts need to know about. However, even on the simple ones, the ones we see, symbols are used rather than words to indicate, for instance, wind direction and force, or that it will rain somewhere. This is to save space, and once one has learned what the symbols and the terms used by the forecasters mean, the charts quickly begin to make sense and become full of interest.

Above: *BBC Television weather map (see symbols, below).* (BBC copyright)
Right: *BBC Television weather map showing isobars and warm and cold fronts.* (BBC copyright)

(15)	Temperature (°C)		Sunny intervals		Sleet
(25)	Sunshine		Rain		Thunderstorm
	Fine-weather cloud		Rain showers and sunny intervals	30 →	Wind speed and direction
	Thick cloud		Snow	FOG	Fog (no symbol)

There is some similarity between a weather chart and a map which shows the heights of hills and mountains. The map will have what are known as contour lines drawn round hills, mountains and high ground, each line bearing a figure in feet or metres showing the height above sea level that the line represents. The nearer the line is to the hill-top or mountain peak, the greater the figure will be.

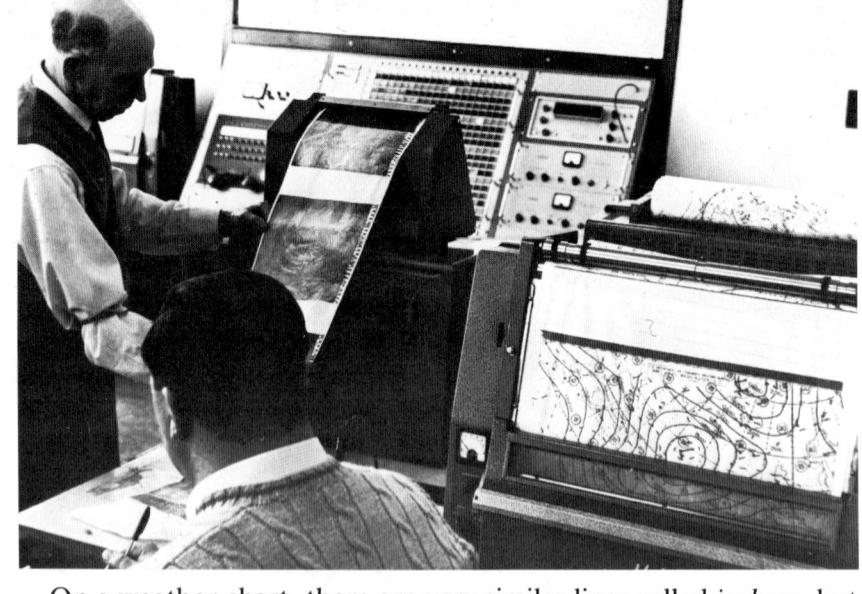

A weather satellite photographs changing cloud formations.

On a weather chart, there are very similar lines called *isobars*, but in this case they surround areas of either high or low pressure, and instead of indicating heights, the figures against them show pressure, measured in millibars. The figures are higher as they approach the centre of a high-pressure area (the mountain peak), which is known as an *anticyclone*, and decrease towards the centre of a low-pressure area, known as a *depression*. A *ridge of high pressure*, often mentioned in forecasts, is really two anticyclones which are linked together by a high-pressure belt of air.

Though figures and symbols are usually used, on the weather maps we see every day the centre point of an anticyclone may carry the word 'high', and a depression may carry the word 'low', both words being short and not taking up much space. Other things such as rain, clouds and snow are represented by small, easily recognisable, drawings. Wind speed (in kilometres per hour), and its direction, are indicated by short straight lines, with other lines branching out from them rather like the feathers of an arrow. One short feather means a wind speed of 5 kph, and one long feather means 10 kph, so two long and one short feather would mean a wind speed of 25 kph (two 10s and a 5). Three long feathers would mean 30 kph, and so on.

In addition to the pressure isobars, there are other lines showing what are known as *warm and cold fronts*. These are points where large masses of cold and warm air come together, and if the difference between their temperatures is great enough it will bring clouds and rain, for the warm air will rise above the cold. Cold fronts are shown as lines which are generally curved and which have black triangles along them, pointing like arrow-heads in the direction the front is moving. Warm fronts have black half-circles instead. In time, two fronts may mingle into a single front, known as an *occlusion*, and this is shown by alternate triangles and half-circles.

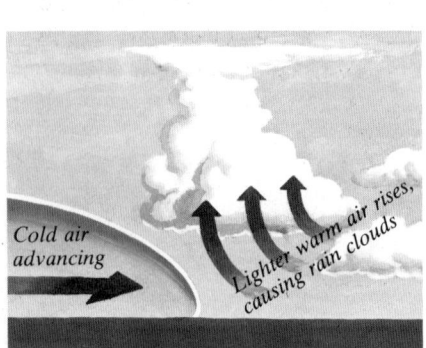

Cold air advancing

Lighter warm air rises, causing rain clouds

How a cold front comes about.

WEATHER CHART	DATE	TIME	DATE	TIME	DATE	TIME	DATE	TIME	DATE	TIME	DATE	TIME	DATE	TIME
RAIN IN INCHES OR MILLIMETRES														
PRESSURE IN MILLIBARS														
TEMPERATURE IN DEGREES F° or C°														
WIND SPEED														

Household barometer.

Thermometer in shade.

Your own weather forecasts

Because the information on them has to be gathered from many sources, and the weather maps themselves take time to prepare, the information on them must always be a little behind the times. They cover, too, a much larger area than a town or village where you may live, so it is useful and interesting to carry out your own observations at home and to keep records of them. To have any value, this must be done regularly – at least once a day, and preferably twice – because things can, as we have seen, change very rapidly, but once a pattern of working has been set, it need not take up too much time.

First of all a chart must be prepared on which can be recorded such things as temperature, barometer readings (pressure), rainfall, and wind speed and direction, and a fixed time each day must be decided on for making the entries. After a while, by looking at the chart, it will be possible to see what combination of the figures you have written down will produce certain types of weather, and watching the sky and the different types of clouds that are forming there will tell you a great deal, too.

A barometer usually carries the words Stormy, Rain, Change, Fair and Very Dry, but there will be a scale with figures on it as well, all round the dial. These show the atmospheric pressure in millibars, the highest number being against Very Dry and the lowest against Stormy. Temperature can be taken from a normal household thermometer (which must not be in full sun), and a jam-jar placed on

the lawn (so that water will not splash into it as it would from a harder surface) will make a good rain gauge.

We have already seen, however, that even a lot of rain will produce so little water that it will be difficult to measure the depth. To get over this, fill the jam jar with exactly 1 inch (or 20 millimetres) of water, and then pour it into another, much narrower, straight-sided jar. The water will come much higher up the sides of this, and the depth can more easily be measured. Mark the measurement on a narrow slip of paper and divide it into ten, also marking each division on the paper. Tape it to the side of the narrow jar, with the lowest mark level with base inside. After rain, pour rainwater from the jam jar into the narrow one and, by counting the divisions from the bottom to the surface of the water, you can see how much has fallen in tenths of an inch (or in millimetres).

For finding out wind direction, a weather vane is not difficult to make out of plywood, painted to protect it from the weather, and for wind speed the Beaufort Scale shown on page 15 should be used.

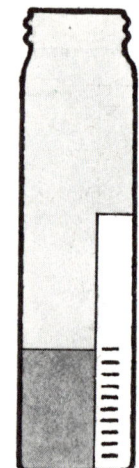
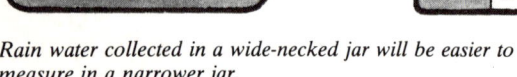

Rain water collected in a wide-necked jar will be easier to measure in a narrower jar.

A wind vane.

Other books you can read:

Frank Mitchell-Christie, PRACTICAL WEATHER FORECASTING, *Luscombe.*

Bill Giles, WEATHER OBSERVATION, *EP Publishing.*

David A. Hardy, AIR AND WEATHER, *World's Work.*

John Hulbert, ALL ABOUT WEATHER, *W. H. Allen.*

Ingrid Holford, GUINNESS BOOK OF WEATHER FACTS AND FEATS, *Guinness Superlatives.*

A. G. Forsdyke, THE WEATHER GUIDE, *Hamlyn All-Colour Paperbacks.*

PRINTED IN BELGIUM BY
INTERNATIONAL BOOK PRODUCTION